JIM HENSON'S MUPPETS™ PRESENT

ROWLF'S VERY OWN FIRST PIANO BOOK

By Lynn Freeman Olson

Edited by Milton Okun

Illustrated by Daryl Kagle

T0044601

ROWLF'S BLUES

By LYNN FREEMAN OLSON

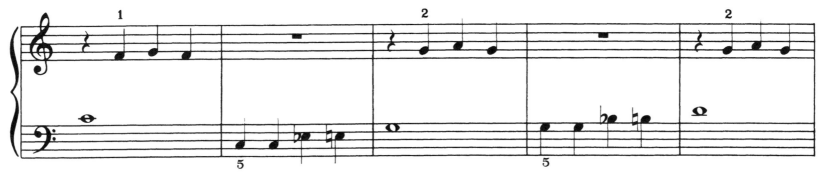

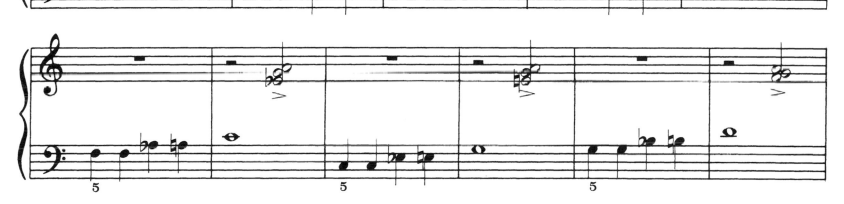

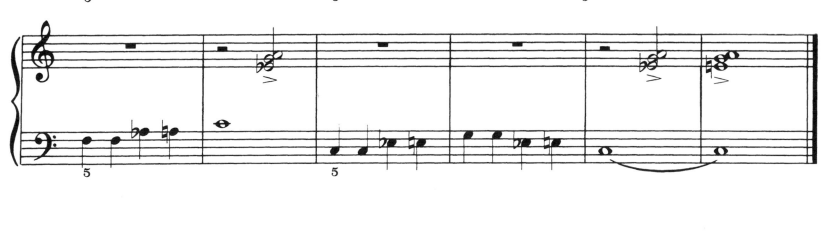

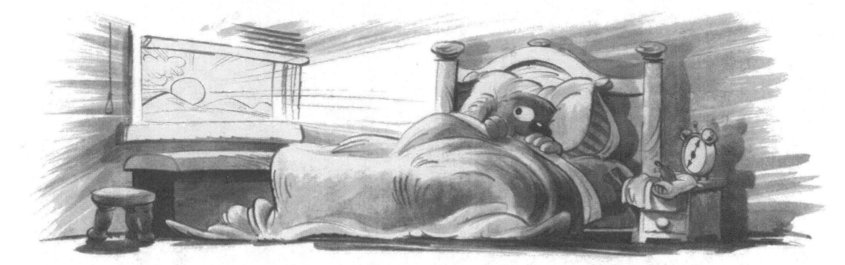

SLEEPY MORNING

By LYNN FREEMAN OLSON

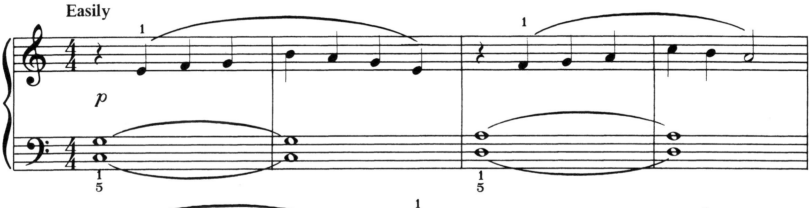

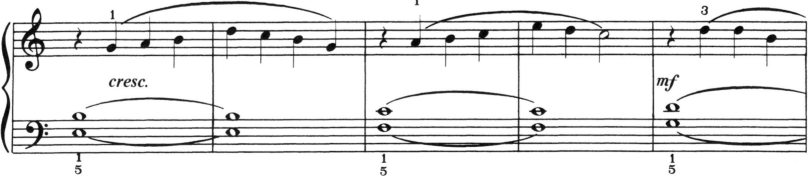

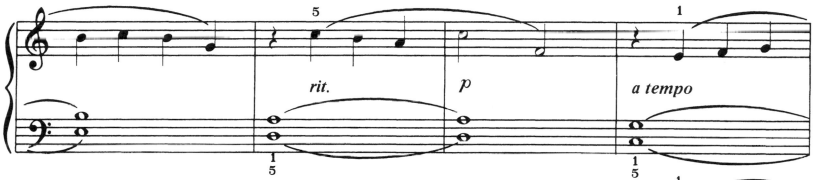

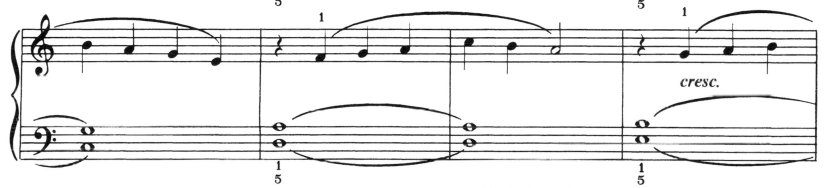

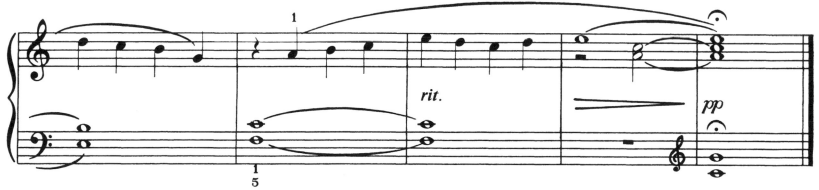

SPELLING LESSON: C A D G

By LYNN FREEMAN OLSON

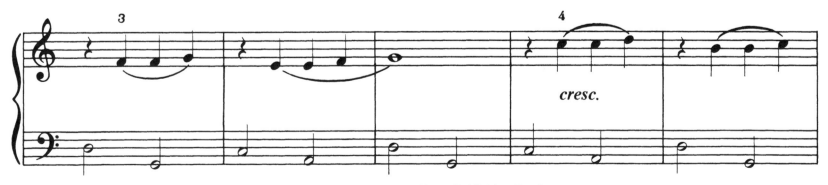

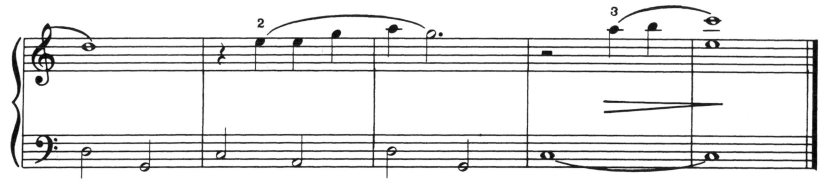

ROWLF'S RAG

By LYNN FREEMAN OLSON

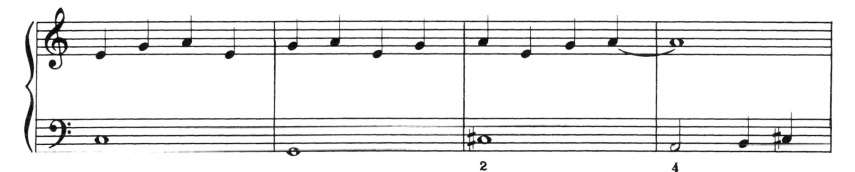

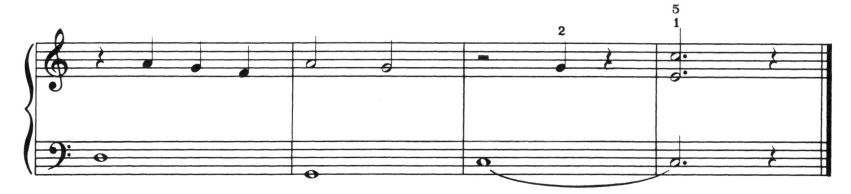

RAINY DAY MOOD

By LYNN FREEMAN OLSON

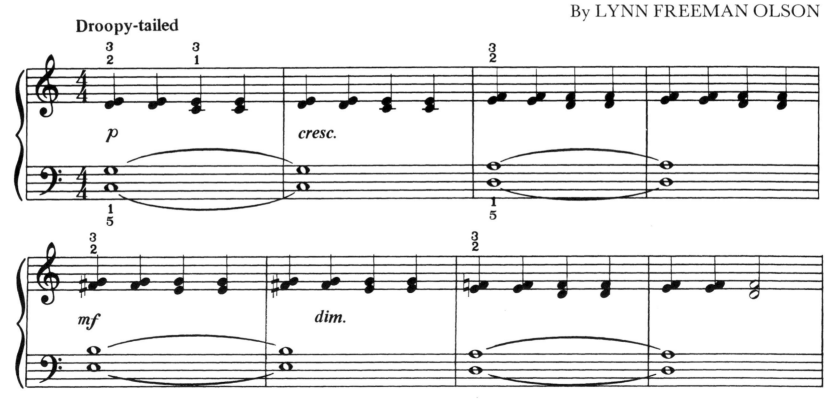

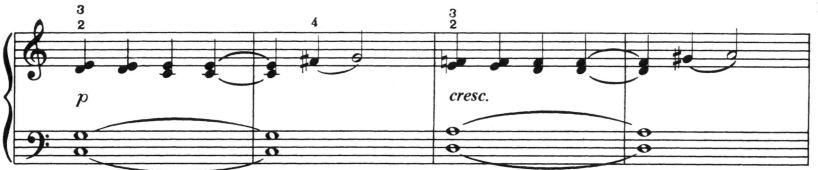

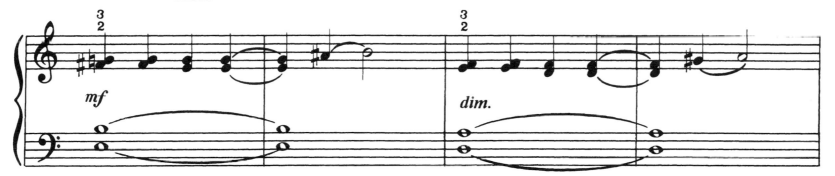

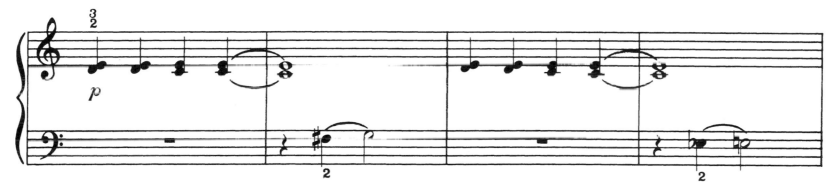

ROWLF'S TUNE

By LYNN FREEMAN OLSON

BLUE NOTES

By LYNN FREEMAN OLSON

MOVING ALONG

By LYNN FREEMAN OLSON

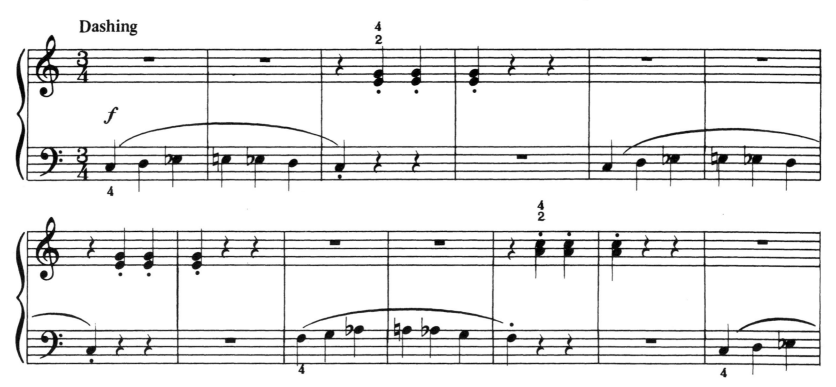

GRASSHOPPERS

By LYNN FREEMAN OLSON

Hoppy, but not fast

A SONG TO YOU

By LYNN FREEMAN OLSON

HAPPY TIMES

By LYNN FREEMAN OLSON

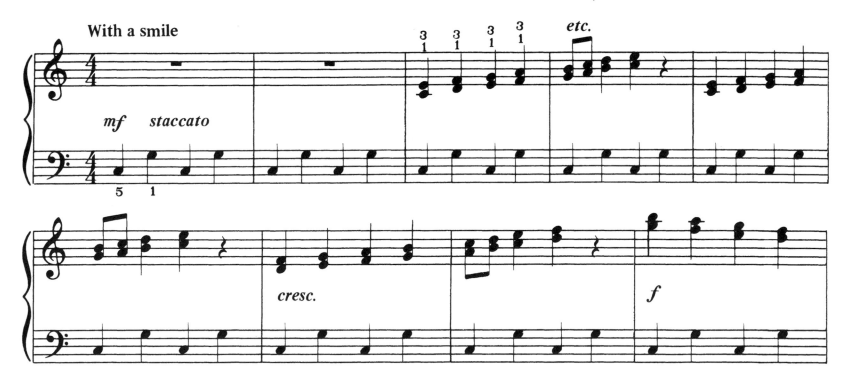

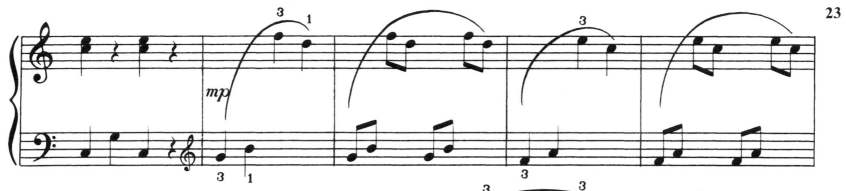

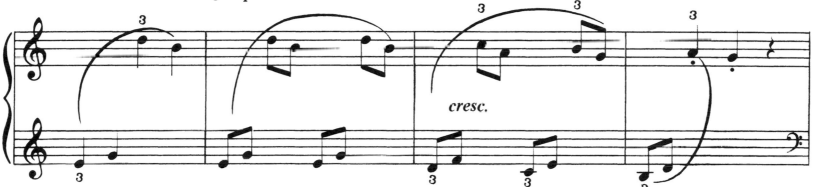